The North
Address Book

Photographs by
Sherman Hines

NIMBUS PUBLISHING LIMITED

Nimbus Publishing Limited
P.O. Box 9301, Station A
Halifax, N.S. B3K 5N5

ISBN 0-921054-48-3
Printed in Hong Kong

A native of Liverpool, Nova Scotia, Sherman
Hines is a graduate of the prestigious Brooks
Institute of Photography in California and a
fellow of the American Society of Photographers.
He has also won the Leonardo da Vinci gold
medal of Philadelphia's Institute for Achievement
of Human Potential and belongs to the very
select Canadian Photographic Art Group. In
1989 he received a gold medal from the National
Association of Photographic Arts.

Hines affinity with the North is well documented
in the hundreds of photographs of that rugged
and fragile land which he has had reproduced in
numerous publications. He attributes his success
in bringing the vast and varied expanse of this
little-known frontier within our grasp to the
hunting and survival skills learned in his youth.

Front-Cover Photo: An igloo made by cutting
blocks of hard snow
Back-Cover Photo: Sundogs, Cambridge Bay,
N.W.T.

Personal Information

Name

Address

City	Prov. / State	Postal Code

Telephone

Business Address

City	Prov. / State	Postal Code

Telephone

Social Security #

Passport #	Expiry Date

Auto	Make	Model	Serial Number

Driving License #	Expiry Date

Credit Cards	Expiry Date

In Case of Emergency Please Notify

Name

Address

City	Prov.	Postal Code	Telephone

Physican

Office Telephone	Home Telephone

Blood Group	Allergies

Frequently Used Telephone Numbers

Name	Telephone

Name and Address	Telephone		Name and Address	Telephone
	Area Code			Area Code
Postal Code			Postal Code	
	Area Code			Area Code
Postal Code			Postal Code	
	Area Code			Area Code
Postal Code			Postal Code	
	Area Code			Area Code
Postal Code			Postal Code	
	Area Code			Area Code
Postal Code			Postal Code	
	Area Code			Area Code
Postal Code			Postal Code	
	Area Code			Area Code
Postal Code			Postal Code	
	Area Code			Area Code
Postal Code			Postal Code	
	Area Code			Area Code
Postal Code			Postal Code	

ctic wild flowers

A

Name and Address	Telephone	Name and Address	Telephone
	Area Code		Area Code
Postal Code		Postal Code	
	Area Code		Area Code
Postal Code		Postal Code	
	Area Code		Area Code
Postal Code		Postal Code	
	Area Code		Area Code
Postal Code		Postal Code	
	Area Code		Area Code
Postal Code		Postal Code	
	Area Code		Area Code
Postal Code		Postal Code	
	Area Code		Area Code
Postal Code		Postal Code	
	Area Code		Area Code
Postal Code		Postal Code	
	Area Code		Area Code
Postal Code		Postal Code	
	Area Code		Area Code
Postal Code		Postal Code	

550 ft. peak at the North Fork Pass, on the Dempster Highway, Yukon

B

Name and Address	Telephone	Name and Address	Telephone
	Area Code		Area Code
Postal Code		Postal Code	
	Area Code		Area Code
Postal Code		Postal Code	
	Area Code		Area Code
Postal Code		Postal Code	
	Area Code		Area Code
Postal Code		Postal Code	
	Area Code		Area Code
Postal Code		Postal Code	
	Area Code		Area Code
Postal Code		Postal Code	
	Area Code		Area Code
Postal Code		Postal Code	
	Area Code		Area Code
Postal Code		Postal Code	
	Area Code		Area Code
Postal Code		Postal Code	

iverboat *Klondike*, Whitehorse, Yukon

C

Name and Address	Telephone	Name and Address	Telephone
	Area Code		Area Code
Postal Code		Postal Code	
	Area Code		Area Code
Postal Code		Postal Code	
	Area Code		Area Code
Postal Code		Postal Code	
	Area Code		Area Code
Postal Code		Postal Code	
	Area Code		Area Code
Postal Code		Postal Code	
	Area Code		Area Code
Postal Code		Postal Code	
	Area Code		Area Code
Postal Code		Postal Code	
	Area Code		Area Code
Postal Code		Postal Code	
	Area Code		Area Code
Postal Code		Postal Code	
	Area Code		Area Code
Postal Code		Postal Code	

g team, Yukon

D

Name and Address	Telephone	Name and Address	Telephone
	Area Code		Area Code
Postal Code		Postal Code	
	Area Code		Area Code
Postal Code		Postal Code	
	Area Code		Area Code
Postal Code		Postal Code	
	Area Code		Area Code
Postal Code		Postal Code	
	Area Code		Area Code
Postal Code		Postal Code	
	Area Code		Area Code
Postal Code		Postal Code	
	Area Code		Area Code
Postal Code		Postal Code	
	Area Code		Area Code
Postal Code		Postal Code	
	Area Code		Area Code
Postal Code		Postal Code	

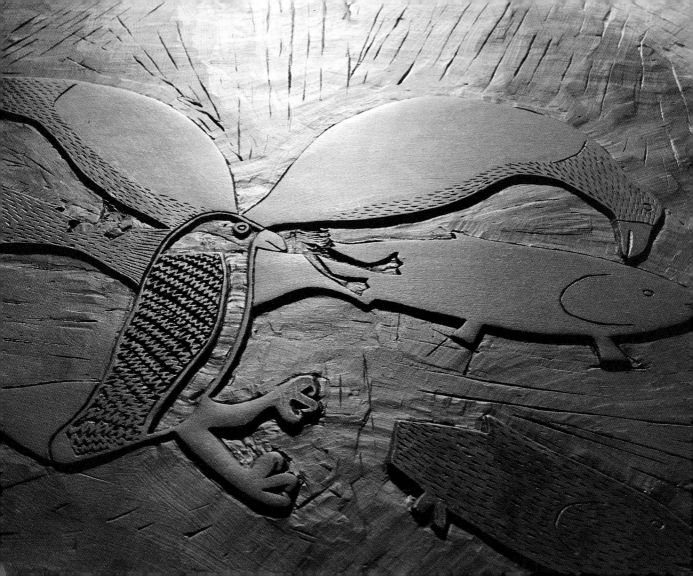

Name and Address	Telephone	Name and Address	Telephone
	Area Code		Area Code
Postal Code		Postal Code	
	Area Code		Area Code
Postal Code		Postal Code	
	Area Code		Area Code
Postal Code		Postal Code	
	Area Code		Area Code
Postal Code		Postal Code	
	Area Code		Area Code
Postal Code		Postal Code	
	Area Code		Area Code
Postal Code		Postal Code	
	Area Code		Area Code
Postal Code		Postal Code	
	Area Code		Area Code
Postal Code		Postal Code	
	Area Code		Area Code
Postal Code		Postal Code	
	Area Code		Area Code
Postal Code		Postal Code	

nestone used in the printmaking process, Cape Dorset, N.W.T.

F

ame and Address	Telephone	Name and Address	Telephone
	Area Code		Area Code
Postal Code		Postal Code	
	Area Code		Area Code
Postal Code		Postal Code	
	Area Code		Area Code
Postal Code		Postal Code	
	Area Code		Area Code
Postal Code		Postal Code	
	Area Code		Area Code
Postal Code		Postal Code	
	Area Code		Area Code
Postal Code		Postal Code	
	Area Code		Area Code
Postal Code		Postal Code	
	Area Code		Area Code
Postal Code		Postal Code	
	Area Code		Area Code
Postal Code		Postal Code	

wson, Yukon, heart of the 1898 Gold Rush

G

Name and Address	Telephone	Name and Address	Telephone
	Area Code		Area Code
Postal Code		Postal Code	
	Area Code		Area Code
Postal Code		Postal Code	
	Area Code		Area Code
Postal Code		Postal Code	
	Area Code		Area Code
Postal Code		Postal Code	
	Area Code		Area Code
Postal Code		Postal Code	
	Area Code		Area Code
Postal Code		Postal Code	
	Area Code		Area Code
Postal Code		Postal Code	
	Area Code		Area Code
Postal Code		Postal Code	
	Area Code		Area Code
Postal Code		Postal Code	

unch on the trail, Atlin, B.C.

H

Name and Address	Telephone	Name and Address	Telephone
	Area Code		Area Code
Postal Code		Postal Code	
	Area Code		Area Code
Postal Code		Postal Code	
	Area Code		Area Code
Postal Code		Postal Code	
	Area Code		Area Code
Postal Code		Postal Code	
	Area Code		Area Code
Postal Code		Postal Code	
	Area Code		Area Code
Postal Code		Postal Code	
	Area Code		Area Code
Postal Code		Postal Code	
	Area Code		Area Code
Postal Code		Postal Code	
	Area Code		Area Code
Postal Code		Postal Code	

rctic wild flowers

I

Name and Address	Telephone	Name and Address	Telephone
	Area Code		Area Code
Postal Code		Postal Code	
	Area Code		Area Code
Postal Code		Postal Code	
	Area Code		Area Code
Postal Code		Postal Code	
	Area Code		Area Code
Postal Code		Postal Code	
	Area Code		Area Code
Postal Code		Postal Code	
	Area Code		Area Code
Postal Code		Postal Code	
	Area Code		Area Code
Postal Code		Postal Code	
	Area Code		Area Code
Postal Code		Postal Code	
	Area Code		Area Code
Postal Code		Postal Code	
	Area Code		Area Code
Postal Code		Postal Code	

ctic ground squirrel, Yukon

J

Name and Address	Telephone	Name and Address	Telephone
	Area Code		Area Code
Postal Code		Postal Code	
	Area Code		Area Code
Postal Code		Postal Code	
	Area Code		Area Code
Postal Code		Postal Code	
	Area Code		Area Code
Postal Code		Postal Code	
	Area Code		Area Code
Postal Code		Postal Code	
	Area Code		Area Code
Postal Code		Postal Code	
	Area Code		Area Code
Postal Code		Postal Code	
	Area Code		Area Code
Postal Code		Postal Code	
	Area Code		Area Code
Postal Code		Postal Code	

ondike River near Rock Creek, -50°C, Yukon

K

ame and Address	Telephone	Name and Address	Telephone
	Area Code		Area Code
Postal Code		Postal Code	
	Area Code		Area Code
Postal Code		Postal Code	
	Area Code		Area Code
Postal Code		Postal Code	
	Area Code		Area Code
Postal Code		Postal Code	
	Area Code		Area Code
Postal Code		Postal Code	
	Area Code		Area Code
Postal Code		Postal Code	
	Area Code		Area Code
Postal Code		Postal Code	
	Area Code		Area Code
Postal Code		Postal Code	
	Area Code		Area Code
Postal Code		Postal Code	

e Penny Ice Cap, Auyuittuq National Park, Cumberland Peninsula, Baffin Island, N.W.T.

L

ame and Address	Telephone	Name and Address	Telephone
	Area Code		Area Code
Postal Code		Postal Code	
	Area Code		Area Code
Postal Code		Postal Code	
	Area Code		Area Code
Postal Code		Postal Code	
	Area Code		Area Code
Postal Code		Postal Code	
	Area Code		Area Code
Postal Code		Postal Code	
	Area Code		Area Code
Postal Code		Postal Code	
	Area Code		Area Code
Postal Code		Postal Code	
	Area Code		Area Code
Postal Code		Postal Code	
	Area Code		Area Code
Postal Code		Postal Code	

ehip, an important source of vitamin C

M

Name and Address	Telephone	Name and Address	Telephone
	Area Code		Area Code
Postal Code		Postal Code	
	Area Code		Area Code
Postal Code		Postal Code	
	Area Code		Area Code
Postal Code		Postal Code	
	Area Code		Area Code
Postal Code		Postal Code	
	Area Code		Area Code
Postal Code		Postal Code	
	Area Code		Area Code
Postal Code		Postal Code	
	Area Code		Area Code
Postal Code		Postal Code	
	Area Code		Area Code
Postal Code		Postal Code	
	Area Code		Area Code
Postal Code		Postal Code	

untain caribou on the crest of Red Mountain, B.C.

N

Name and Address	Telephone	Name and Address	Telephone
	Area Code		Area Code
Postal Code		Postal Code	
	Area Code		Area Code
Postal Code		Postal Code	
	Area Code		Area Code
Postal Code		Postal Code	
	Area Code		Area Code
Postal Code		Postal Code	
	Area Code		Area Code
Postal Code		Postal Code	
	Area Code		Area Code
Postal Code		Postal Code	
	Area Code		Area Code
Postal Code		Postal Code	
	Area Code		Area Code
Postal Code		Postal Code	
	Area Code		Area Code
Postal Code		Postal Code	

Name and Address	Telephone	Name and Address	Telephone
	Area Code		Area Code
Postal Code		Postal Code	
	Area Code		Area Code
Postal Code		Postal Code	
	Area Code		Area Code
Postal Code		Postal Code	
	Area Code		Area Code
Postal Code		Postal Code	
	Area Code		Area Code
Postal Code		Postal Code	
	Area Code		Area Code
Postal Code		Postal Code	
	Area Code		Area Code
Postal Code		Postal Code	
	Area Code		Area Code
Postal Code		Postal Code	
	Area Code		Area Code
Postal Code		Postal Code	

ffed grouse, Yukon

P

Name and Address	Telephone	Name and Address	Telephone
	Area Code		Area Code
Postal Code		Postal Code	
	Area Code		Area Code
Postal Code		Postal Code	
	Area Code		Area Code
Postal Code		Postal Code	
	Area Code		Area Code
Postal Code		Postal Code	
	Area Code		Area Code
Postal Code		Postal Code	
	Area Code		Area Code
Postal Code		Postal Code	
	Area Code		Area Code
Postal Code		Postal Code	
	Area Code		Area Code
Postal Code		Postal Code	
	Area Code		Area Code
Postal Code		Postal Code	

ctic cotton grass, Pond Inlet, N.W.T.

Q

ame and Address	Telephone	Name and Address	Telephone
	Area Code		Area Code
Postal Code		Postal Code	
	Area Code		Area Code
Postal Code		Postal Code	
	Area Code		Area Code
Postal Code		Postal Code	
	Area Code		Area Code
Postal Code		Postal Code	
	Area Code		Area Code
Postal Code		Postal Code	
	Area Code		Area Code
Postal Code		Postal Code	
	Area Code		Area Code
Postal Code		Postal Code	
	Area Code		Area Code
Postal Code		Postal Code	
	Area Code		Area Code
Postal Code		Postal Code	

ldren of Pelly Bay, Simpson Peninsula, N.W.T.

R

ame and Address	Telephone	Name and Address	Telephone
	Area Code		Area Code
Postal Code		Postal Code	
	Area Code		Area Code
Postal Code		Postal Code	
	Area Code		Area Code
Postal Code		Postal Code	
	Area Code		Area Code
Postal Code		Postal Code	
	Area Code		Area Code
Postal Code		Postal Code	
	Area Code		Area Code
Postal Code		Postal Code	
	Area Code		Area Code
Postal Code		Postal Code	
	Area Code		Area Code
Postal Code		Postal Code	
	Area Code		Area Code
Postal Code		Postal Code	

ntyre Creek, Klondike Highway, north of Whitehorse, Yukon

S

Name and Address	Telephone	Name and Address	Telephone
	Area Code		Area Code
Postal Code		Postal Code	
	Area Code		Area Code
Postal Code		Postal Code	
	Area Code		Area Code
Postal Code		Postal Code	
	Area Code		Area Code
Postal Code		Postal Code	
	Area Code		Area Code
Postal Code		Postal Code	
	Area Code		Area Code
Postal Code		Postal Code	
	Area Code		Area Code
Postal Code		Postal Code	
	Area Code		Area Code
Postal Code		Postal Code	
	Area Code		Area Code
Postal Code		Postal Code	
	Area Code		Area Code
Postal Code		Postal Code	

nuk, the Inuit name for polar bear.

T

Name and Address	Telephone	Name and Address	Telephone
	Area Code		Area Code
	Postal Code		Postal Code
	Area Code		Area Code
	Postal Code		Postal Code
	Area Code		Area Code
	Postal Code		Postal Code
	Area Code		Area Code
	Postal Code		Postal Code
	Area Code		Area Code
	Postal Code		Postal Code
	Area Code		Area Code
	Postal Code		Postal Code
	Area Code		Area Code
	Postal Code		Postal Code
	Area Code		Area Code
	Postal Code		Postal Code
	Area Code		Area Code
	Postal Code		Postal Code

Name and Address	Telephone	Name and Address	Telephone
	Area Code		Area Code
Postal Code		Postal Code	
	Area Code		Area Code
Postal Code		Postal Code	
	Area Code		Area Code
Postal Code		Postal Code	
	Area Code		Area Code
Postal Code		Postal Code	
	Area Code		Area Code
Postal Code		Postal Code	
	Area Code		Area Code
Postal Code		Postal Code	
	Area Code		Area Code
Postal Code		Postal Code	
	Area Code		Area Code
Postal Code		Postal Code	
	Area Code		Area Code
Postal Code		Postal Code	

eberg, Cumberland Sound, N.W.T.

V

Name and Address	Telephone	Name and Address	Telephone
	Area Code		Area Code
Postal Code		Postal Code	
	Area Code		Area Code
Postal Code		Postal Code	
	Area Code		Area Code
Postal Code		Postal Code	
	Area Code		Area Code
Postal Code		Postal Code	
	Area Code		Area Code
Postal Code		Postal Code	
	Area Code		Area Code
Postal Code		Postal Code	
	Area Code		Area Code
Postal Code		Postal Code	
	Area Code		Area Code
Postal Code		Postal Code	
	Area Code		Area Code
Postal Code		Postal Code	

rctic poppies, Pond Inlet, N.W.T.

W

Name and Address	Telephone	Name and Address	Telephone
	Area Code		Area Code
Postal Code		Postal Code	
	Area Code		Area Code
Postal Code		Postal Code	
	Area Code		Area Code
Postal Code		Postal Code	
	Area Code		Area Code
Postal Code		Postal Code	
	Area Code		Area Code
Postal Code		Postal Code	
	Area Code		Area Code
Postal Code		Postal Code	
	Area Code		Area Code
Postal Code		Postal Code	
	Area Code		Area Code
Postal Code		Postal Code	
	Area Code		Area Code
Postal Code		Postal Code	

ribou, northern Québec

XYZ

Emergency Telephone Numbers

Name	Area Code	Number	Details
Police			
Ambulance			
Fire Department			
Hospital			

Pine cones, needles, lichen and twigs at the 12-Kilometre Camp, Atlin Lake, B.C.

Time Zones and Area Codes

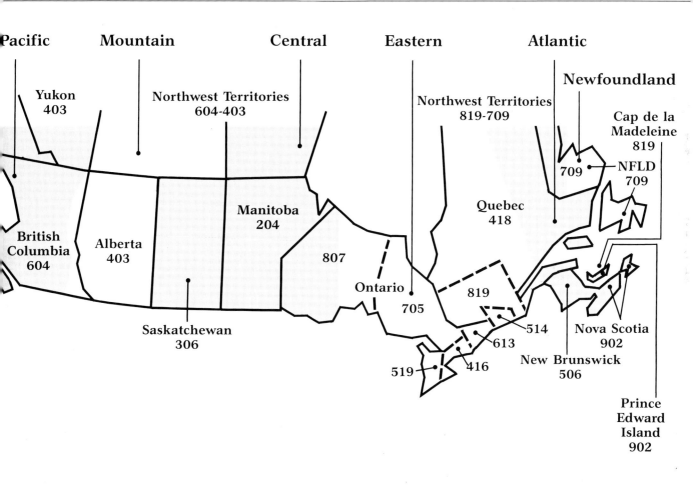

Pacific   Mountain   Central   Eastern   Atlantic

Newfoundland

Yukon
403

Northwest Territories
604-403

Northwest Territories
819-709

Cap de la
Madeleine
819

709 — NFLD
709

Quebec
418

Manitoba
204

British
Columbia
604

Alberta
403

807

Ontario
705

519

416

613

519

514

819

New Brunswick
506

Nova Scotia
902

Saskatchewan
306

Prince
Edward
Island
902

robisher Bay, Baffin Island, N.W.T.